'GET A GRIP ON YOURSELF'

Copyright 1990 by
Hands on Graphics
Vashon Island, WA 98070

ISBN-0-910303-20-7

YOU'VE GONE OUT ON THE TOWN UNTIL YOU'RE BROKE . . .

YOU'VE THROWN MONEY AWAY ON DATING
SERVICES . . .

AND MOST NIGHTS YOU STILL SPEND ALONE . . .

WHEN YOU MEET SOMEONE NEW, YOU HAVE TO
PLAY 20 QUESTIONS . . .

THERE IS DEFINITELY A CHANGE IN THE TYPE OF QUESTIONS THAT ARE RELEVANT.

EVEN IF THE ANSWERS ARE RIGHT, YOU STILL <u>MUST</u> USE THOSE RUBBER THINGS.

AND IF ONE SHOULD FAIL . . . THE CONSEQUENCES CAN BE DEVASTATING.

SO YOU CAN CONTINUE TO SIT AT HOME ALONE . . .

OR GO OUT AND TAKE YOUR CHANCES . . .

OR YOU COULD BE 100% SAFE, BY PRACTICING
VERY <u>VERY</u> SAFE SEX . . .

WHAT, YOU ARE ASKING IS VERY <u>VERY</u> SAFE SEX.

IT'S FINE FUN WITH FROLICKING FRIEDA AND HER
FIVE FINGER FRIENDS.

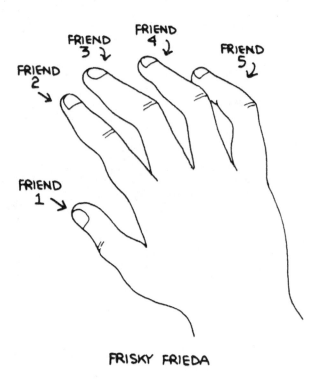

FRISKY FRIEDA

THIS MEANS SOME ADAPTATIONS. FIRST YOU'LL
WANT TO GET RID OF ANY CLUNKY JEWELRY.

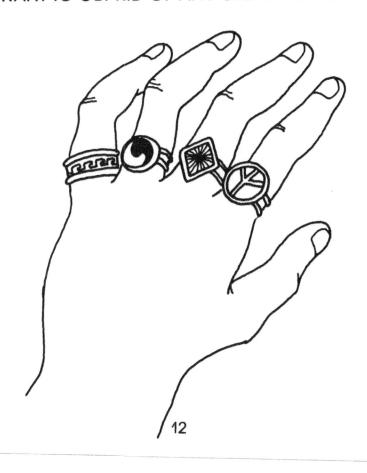

YOU MAY WANT TO START AN EXERCISE PROGRAM.

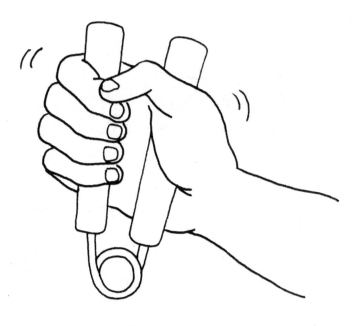

BUY THE PROPER CREAMS & GELS . . .

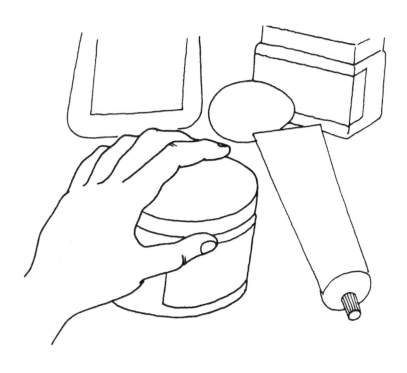

IT'S CHEAPER THAN A NIGHT ON THE TOWN . . .

YOU'RE NEVER TOO LARGE

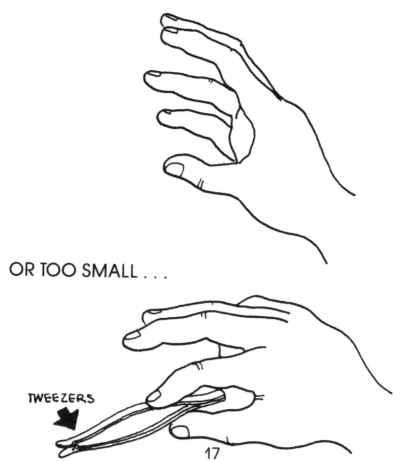

OR TOO SMALL . . .

TWEEZERS

17

YOU DON'T HAVE TO GET DRESSED UP . . .

OR BATHE AND CUT YOUR HAIR . . .

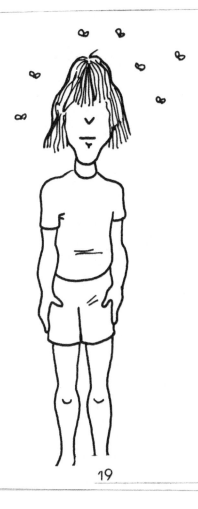

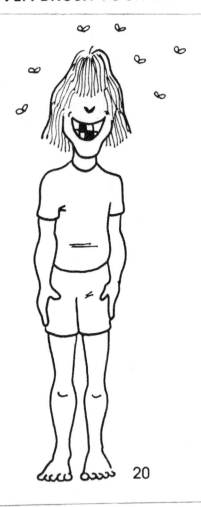

20

YOU CAN PRACTICE VERY <u>VERY</u> SAFE SEX
WHENEVER THE MOOD STRIKES YOU . . .

21

YOU MAY WANT TO GIVE FRISKY FRIEDA SOME
PERSONALITY . . .

PERHAPS START WITH SOME EYES . . .

PERHAPS A TATTOO . . .

LIPS AND EYELASHES HELP . . .

PERHAPS A NOSE . . .

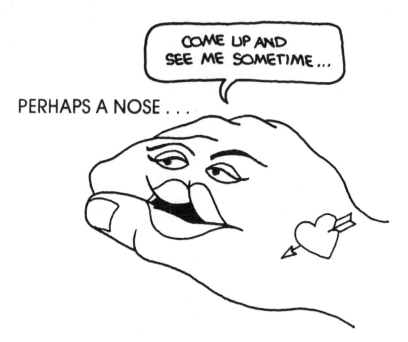

EYEBROWS ADD EXPRESSION . . .

YOU CAN HAVE A THREESOME . . .

BE DARING . . .

IN THE MORNING YOU CAN HAVE COFFEE
TOGETHER . . .

YOU'LL HAVE TO STAY IN CONTROL OF JEALOUSY
AND RIVALRY . . .

BE CAREFUL WITH POST-COITAL CIGARETTES . . .

YOU MAY CONSIDER TAKING A JUGGLING CLASS

DIFFERENT SCENARIOS CAN BE ACTED OUT FOR
YOUR PLEASURE . . .

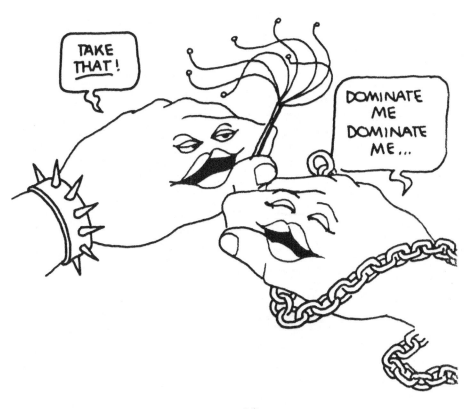

PLAY ACTING IS AN OPTION. YOU CAN TRY ALL
DIFFERENT ROLES . . .

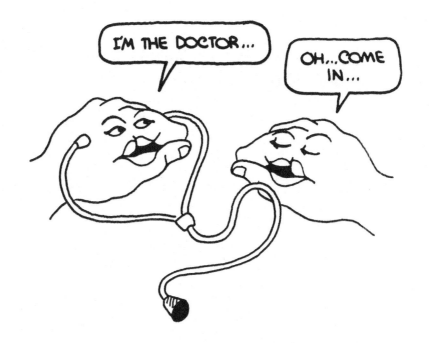

AS YOU CAN SEE . . . THERE ARE FEW LIMITS TO THE VARIATIONS OF VERY <u>VERY</u> SAFE SEX . . .

HOWEVER, YOU MAY FIND SOME SIDE EFFECTS DEVELOPING . . .

YOU MAY FIND YOU DON'T LIKE HOT DOGS AS MUCH ANYMORE . . .

YOU MAY BECOME A VEGETARIAN . . .

YOU MAY FIND YOURSELF GOING THROUGH A LOT
OF RAZORS . . .

33

YOUR FRIENDS MAY RUN INTO PROBLEMS . . .

THIS CAN PLAY HELL WITH YOUR EYE-HAND
COORDINATION . . .

YOU MAY FIND YOURSELF HAVING TO TAKE COLD
SHOWERS AT ANY TIME . . .

YOU'LL TOSS AND TURN AT NIGHT UNABLE TO KEEP
YOUR HANDS UNDER THE COVER . . .

FINALLY GIVING IN, YOU'LL SLEEP AN EXHAUSTED
SLEEP . . .

AT THIS POINT YOU MAY THINK IT'S TIME TO GET A
REAL PARTNER . . . BUT WHO . . . ?

THE ANSWER IS OBVIOUS . . .

SOMEONE ELSE WHO PRACTICES VERY <u>VERY</u> SAFE SEX.

SO A HAPPY ENDING . . . YOU'VE FOUND A
COMPATABLE PARTNER . . . YOU HAVE LOVE,
UNDERSTANDING . . .

AND ALL OF YOU ARE <u>VERY</u> <u>VERY</u> SAFE.